CONFUCIUS

The Great Digest

The Unwobbling Pivot

The Analects

Stone Text from
rubbings supplied by
WILLIAM HAWLEY

A Note on the
Stone Editions by
ACHILLES FANG

TRANSLATION & COMMENTARY BY

EZRA POUND

CONFUCIUS

THE GREAT DIGEST
THE UNWOBBLING PIVOT
THE ANALECTS

A NEW DIRECTIONS BOOK

 Library of Congress Catalog Card Number: 74-87911. The translation of *The Analects* first appeared in *Hudson Review,* Spring-Summer, 1950, and later in the "Square $ Series" pamphlet of 1951. *The Great Digest* first appeared as "Ta Hio: The Great Learning" in a University of Washington Book Store pamphlet, Seattle, 1928; then in a New Directions pamphlet in 1939; then in the ND Direction Series pamphlet, "The Great Digest & Unwobbling Pivot," in 1947; and in the first ND "Stone Classics" edition in 1951. *The Unwobbling Pivot* first appeared in the Direction pamphlet of 1947. Manufactured in the United States of America. First published as New Directions Paperbook 285 in 1969. Published simultaneously in Canada by McClelland & Stewart Limited. New Directions Books are published for James Laughlin by New Directions Publishing Corporation, 333 Sixth Avenue, New York 10014.

CONTENTS

An Edition

for

Walter de Rachewiltz

A NOTE ON THE STONE-CLASSICS

> and the books were incised in stone
> 46 tablets set up at the door of the college
> — *Canto LIV* (*page* 27)

In order to establish a standard text of the corpus of Confucian classics, several Chinese dynasties had them incised on stone tablets, which were placed in the Imperial Academy in the metropolis. The editio princeps was produced in the latter days of the Han dynasty, between 175 and 183 A.D. But the stones had to go the way of all books:

> And the 46 tablets that stood there in Lo Yang
> were broken and built into Foé's temple (Foés,
> that is goddam bhuddists.)
> this was under Hou-chi the she empress.
> — *Canto LIV* (*page* 30)

This refers to the year 518 A.D. At present some three hundred fragments of the 46 tablets are known to exist.

The immediately succeeding dynasty, Wei, set up its Stone-Classics sometime between 240 and 249 A.D. by the side of the Han stones at Lo-yang. The unique feature of the Wei stones is that they are inscribed with three styles of calligraphy. Of the original 35 stones a little over 140 fragments still exist.

Passing over the putative stones of the Chin and Toba-Wei dynasties, we come to the great T'ang dynasty. As the Chinese text printed in this book is derived from the T'ang stones, the second part of this note will discuss them in detail.

The short-lived dynasty of Shu (present Ssuch'uan) started its Stone-Classics in 938 A.D.; the work was completed by the Sung in 1124 A.D., long after that minor dynasty (capital: Ch'eng-tu) had perished. Unlike the preceding classics, the Shu classics comprised all the 13, for which more than a thousand stones were needed. Strangely, not a fragment is extant; there are, however, quite a number of their rubbings still available. Incidentally, it was about this time that the Confucian classics began to be printed from wood-blocks.

The Sung, in spite of internal dissensions and barbarian incursions, produced their Stone-Classics twice. It took them 19 years (1042-1061 A.D.) to bring out 9 classics at K'ai-feng. It is not recorded how many stones were needed; only a few fragments are still extant. After they had moved their capital to present Hang-chou, they set up 6 classics and a portion of the Li-chi (Li-ki), including Chung-yung and Ta-hsio. The work took them more than a generation (1135-1177 A.D.). There still exist 86 stones; there is no means of determining the original number of the stones.

Finally, the emperor Ch'ien-lung of the Ch'ing (Manchu) dynasty set up, 1791-1794 A.D., 189 stones inscribed with the text of all the 13 classics. They are still preserved in Peking (see photo on jacket).

The Stone-Classics of the T'ang dynasty, from a rubbing of which the Chinese text of this book is derived, were begun in 833 A.D. and completed in 837; they originally comprised 12 classics, the missing 13th being the Book of Mencius, which had not then acquired the status of a Confucian classic. The text and apparatus criticus, 650, 252 characters in all, took 227 stones, each measuring 6 feet in height and over 2 feet in width. Originally set up in the Imperial Academy in Ch'ang-an (present Hsi-an), these stones have weathered fairly well; except for a few stones which suffered damage in the earthquake of 1555, they are still preserved intact in Hsi-an.

When Chu Hsi lifted chapter 31 (Chung-yung) and 42 (Ta-hsio) out of the Li-ki to make a Confucian quartet (he himself called it Ssu-shu, 'Four Books') by joining them with the Analects of Confucius and the Book of Mencius, he rearranged the sequence of the Ta-hsio text. Mr. Pound's translation follows Chu Hsi's edition; the text had to be re-edited (a mere scissors-&-paste job). As for Chung-yung, no juggling was needed. There are some minor textual variations in both texts between the T'ang reading and the Chu Hsi reading; they are, however, so unimportant that no retouching was deemed necessary.

It should be noted that most of the given names of T'ang emperors preceding Wen-tsung, in whose reign the Stone-Classics were made, are written minus the last stroke; e.g. [illegible] for 民 , because 世民 was the given name of T'ai-tsung. The same applies to compound characters containing imperial names.

The preface to the Ch'ing Stone-Classics, written in 1794 *by Ch'ien-lung (who lived* 1711-1799 *and reigned* 1736-1795), *runs as follows:*

". . . It was Chiang Heng who wrote down the text of these classics; he offered his calligraphy to the throne in

1740. As there were some minor errors in it, I made the Academicians go through it. After which I had it stored in the high halls of Mou-ch'in-tien (in the palace) for the past fifty-odd years; meanwhile I forgot their existence. Some years ago, the editors of the second series of the Shih-ch'ü pao-chi catalogue called my attention to Chiang Heng's calligraphy, when I was delighted and said to myself: 'Indeed! indeed! This cannot be considered as an ordinary sort of calligraphy in which I may take pleasure in times of leisure. No, it must be engraved on stone and placed in the imperial academy, to serve as a memento for the future of how I revered learning and esteemed the process (*tao*). Classics are the norm, the process; and a norm never varies and the process is what is constant, for Heaven and the process never change. These words of Tung Chung-shu hit the mark.'

It was the Han who first set up their 'one-character' stones; then the Wei carried on the tradition with theirs written in three sorts of characters. Of these two, however, we lack detailed information. Stone-Classics were also made by the T'ang and the Sung, both Northern and Southern; they are either erroneous or incomplete . . . .

Old as I am, I am still avid of learning and never relent. I blush to think how little I know. But I must congratulate myself upon having set up these stones in the imperial academy; for they, a work done at the opportune moment, embody the tradition of the sages and stand as a norm for the future. They will serve as a guide for scholars. Chiang Heng's assiduity has now borne fruit.

As for the commentaries transmitted from the past dynasties, they have now usurped the place of the text itself. There is so much controversy and polemic over them; moreover, they are so profuse and prolix. It was, therefore, quite right of Chiang Heng to write down the text only. Some may object to this, alleging that the text cannot be understood without the commentary. My answer is that it would be far better to let the text explain itself than to explain it by means of the commentary. If a student concentrates and uses his mind, he will discover the process (*tao*) between the lines. If he compares the text of the six classics with each other, he will be able to get to the fons et origo and unravel the mystery. It all depends on his labor and intelligence. Moreover, the 13 classics with running commentary that I had reprinted from wood-blocks are still abundantly available."

—Achilles Fang

TA HSIO
THE GREAT DIGEST

NOTE

Starting at the bottom as market inspector, having risen to be Prime Minister, Confucius is more concerned with the necessities of government, and of governmental administration than any other philosopher. He had two thousand years of documented history behind him which he condensed so as to render it useful to men in high official position, not making a mere collection of anecdotes as did Herodotus.

His analysis of why the earlier great emperors had been able to govern greatly was so sound that every durable dynasty, since his time, has risen on a Confucian design and been initiated by a group of Confucians. China was tranquil when her rulers understood these few pages. When the principles here defined were neglected, dynasties waned and chaos ensued. The proponents of a world order will neglect at their peril the study of the only process that has repeatedly proved its efficiency as social coordinate.

TERMINOLOGY

示 The light descending (from the sun, moon and stars.) To be watched as component in ideograms indicating spirits, rites, ceremonies.

明 The sun and moon, the total light process, the radiation, reception and reflection of light; hence, the intelligence. Bright, brightness, shining. Refer to Scotus Erigena, Grosseteste and the notes on light in my *Cavalcanti*.

誠 "Sincerity." The precise definition of the word, pictorially the sun's lance coming to rest on the precise spot verbally. The righthand half of this compound means: to perfect, bring to focus.

The eye (at the right) looking straight into the heart.

What results, i.e., the action resultant from this straight gaze into the heart. The "know thyself" carried into action. Said action also serving to clarify the self knowledge. To translate this simply as "virtue" is on a par with translating rhinoceros, fox and giraffe indifferently by "quadruped" or "animal."

The man in two successive positions. Serves as prefix to indicate motion or action.

彳

The will, the direction of the will, *directio voluntatis*, the officer standing over the heart.

志

To succeed in due hour. Prefix action taking effect at the sun's turn.

Fidelity to the given word. The man here standing by his word.

Humanitas, humanity, in the full sense of the word, "manhood." The man and his full contents.

仁

The process. Footprints and the foot carrying the head; the head conducting the feet, an orderly movement under lead of the intelligence.

TERMINOLOGY

This phrase—nourishing, supporting the destiny—should be compared with the *Odyssey*, I, 34.

鬼

This ideogram for a spirit contains two elements to be watched.

厶

One readily sees the similarity of this element to the bent heraldic arm of Armstrong and Strongi'tharm. I have never found it in composition save where there is indication of energy, I think we may say, a source of personally directed energy.

儿

The running legs indicate rapid motion or at least the capacity for motion.

THE STONE-CLASSICS title refers to the Nineteenth Roll of the book of *CEREMONIES,* and divides the Great Learning into 42 sections. Notes from E.P.'s earlier edition are left where they were.

CHU HSI'S PREFACE

My master the Philosopher Ch'eng says: The Great Learning, Great Digest, is the testament of Confucius, transmitted, the initial study for whomso would pass the gate into virtue. If we today can see how the men of old went about their study, it is due solely to the conservation of these strips of bamboo; the Analects and the Book of Mencius are subsequent.

He who studies must start from this meridian and study with warm precision; cutting to this homely pattern he will not botch.

禮記卷第十九

大學第四十二

鄭氏注

大學之道在明明德在親

CONFUCIUS' TEXT

I.

The great learning [adult study, grinding the corn in the head's mortar to fit it for use] takes root in clarifying the way wherein the intelligence increases through the process of looking straight into one's own heart and acting on the results; it is rooted in watching with affection the way people grow;

民在止於至善知止而后
有定定而后能靜靜而后
能安安而后能慮慮而后
能得物有夲末事有終始
知所先後則近道矣古之
欲明明德於天下者先治

it is rooted in coming to rest, being at ease in perfect equity.

2.

Know the point of rest and then have an orderly mode of procedure; having this orderly procedure one can "grasp the azure," that is, take hold of a clear concept; holding a clear concept one can be at peace [internally], being thus calm one can keep one's head in moments of danger; he who can keep his head in the presence of a tiger is qualified to come to his deed in due hour.

3.

Things have roots and branches; affairs have scopes and beginnings. To know what precedes and what follows, is nearly as good as having a head and feet.

Mencius' epistemology starts from this verse.

4.

The men of old wanting to clarify and diffuse throughout the empire that light which comes from looking straight into the heart and then acting, first set up good government

其國欲治其國者先齊其
家欲齊其家者先脩其身
欲脩其身者先正其心欲
正其心者先誠其意欲誠
其意者先致其知致知在
格物物格而后知至知至

in their own states; wanting good government in their states, they first established order in their own families; wanting order in the home, they first disciplined themselves; desiring self-discipline, they rectified their own hearts; and wanting to rectify their hearts, they sought precise verbal definitions of their inarticulate thoughts [the tones given off by the heart]; wishing to attain precise verbal definitions, they set to extend their knowledge to the utmost. This completion of knowledge is rooted in sorting things into organic categories.

Confucius' Text

5.

When things had been classified in organic categories, knowledge moved toward fulfillment; given the extreme knowable points,

而后意誠意誠而后心正
心正而后身脩身脩而后
家齊家齊而后國治國治
而后天下平自天子以至
於庶人壹是皆以脩身爲
本其本亂而末治者否矣

the inarticulate thoughts were defined with precision [the sun's lance coming to rest on the precise spot verbally]. Having attained this precise verbal definition [*aliter*, this sincerity], they then stabilized their hearts, they disciplined themselves; having attained self-discipline, they set their own houses in order; having order in their own homes, they brought good government to their own states; and when their states were well governed, the empire was brought into equilibrium.

Confucius' Text

6.

From the Emperor, Son of Heaven, down to the common man, singly and all together, this self-discipline is the root.

7.

If the root be in confusion, nothing will be well governed.

其所厚者薄而其所薄者
厚未之有也康誥曰克明
德大甲曰顧諟天之明命
帝典曰克明峻德皆自明
也湯之盤銘曰苟日新日
日新又日新康誥曰作新

The solid cannot be swept away as trivial, nor can trash be established as solid. It just doesn't happen.

"Take not cliff for morass and treacherous bramble."

The preceding is the first chapter of the canon containing Confucius' words as Tseng Tsze has handed them down. Now follow ten chapters of Tseng's thoughts as his disciples recorded them. In the oldest copies there was a certain confusion due to the shuffling of the original bamboo tablets. Now, basing myself on Ch'eng's conclusions, and having reexamined the classic text, I have arranged them as follows. ("On the left," in the Chinese method of writing.) —Chu Hsi.

明

TSENG'S COMMENT

I

1.

It is said in the K'ang Proclamation: He showed his intelligence by acting straight from the heart.

2.

It is said in the Great Announcement: He contemplated the luminous

decree of heaven, and found the precise word wherewith to define it.

Tseng's Comment

3.

It is said in the Canon of the Emperor (Yau): His intelligence shone vital over the hill-crest, he clarified the high-reaching virtue, *id est*, that action which is due to direct self-knowledge.

4.

All these statements proceed from the ideogram of the sun and moon standing together [that is, from the ideogram which expresses the total light process].

明

This is the first chapter of the comment giving the gist (sorting out the grist) of the expressions: Make clear the intelligence by looking straight into the heart and then acting. Clarify the intelligence in straight action.

II

日日新

1.

In letters of gold on T'ang's bath-tub:

As the sun makes it new
Day by day make it new
Yet again make it new.

2.

It is said in the K'ang Proclamation:
He is risen, renewing the people.

3.

The *Odes* say:

Although Chou was an ancient kingdom
The celestial destiny
Came again down on it NEW.

Tseng's Comment

—*Shi King*, III, 1, 1, 1.
(*Decade of King Wen*)

民詩曰周雖舊邦其命惟
新是故君子無所不用其
極詩云邦畿千里維民所
止詩云緡蠻黃鳥止于丘
隅子曰於止知其所止可
以人而不如鳥乎詩云穆

4.

Hence the man in whom speaks the voice of his forebears cuts no log that he does not make fit to be roof-tree [does nothing that he does not bring to a maximum, that he does not carry through to a finish].

Tseng's Comment

This is the second chapter of the comment containing and getting the grist of the phrase: Renew the people.
Ideogram: axe, tree and wood-pile.

新

III

1.

The *Book of Poems* says:
The royal domain is of 1000 *li*
Thither the people would fly to its rest
[*would hew out its resting place*].

—*Shi King*, IV, 3, 3, 4.

2.

The *Book of Poems* says:
The twittering yellow bird,
The bright silky warbler
Talkative as a cricket
Comes to rest in the hollow corner of the hill.

—*Shi King*, II, 8, 6, 2.

Kung said: comes to its rest, alights, knows what its rest is, what its ease is. Is man, for all his wit, less wise than this bird of the yellow plumage that he should not know his resting place or fix the point of his aim?

穆文王於緝熙敬止爲人
君止於仁爲人臣止於敬
爲人子止於孝爲人父止
於慈與國人交止於信詩
云瞻彼淇澳菉竹猗猗有
斐君子如切如磋如琢如

3.

The *Odes* say:

As a field of grain
White-topped in even order,
The little flowing ears of grain
Bending in white, even order,
So glorious was King Wan,
Coherent, splendid and reverent
In his comings to rest, in his bournes.

—*Shi King*, III, 1, 1, 4.

Tseng's Comment

As prince he came to rest in humanity, in the full human qualities, in his manhood;
As a minister, in respect;
As a son, in filial devotion;
As a father in carrying kindliness down into particular acts, and in relation to the people, in fidelity to his given word.

4.

The *Odes* say:

Cast your eye on Ch'i river,
The slow water winding
Bright reflecting the shaggy bamboo;
Shaggy green are the flowing leaves,
Shaggy the bamboo above it,
Our Lord has so many talents
As we cut,
As we file,
As we carve the jade and grind it,

磨瑟兮僩兮赫兮喧兮有
斐君子終不可諠兮如切
如磋者道學也如琢如磨
者自脩也瑟兮僩兮者恂
慄也赫兮喧兮者威儀也
有斐君子終不可諠兮者

Firm in decision, Oh!
On guard against calumny
and its makers, oh!
Splendid, oh! oh!
His voice our impulse, Aye!
A prince of many talents, who will
carry through to the end,
Who will not go back on his word.

—*Shi King*, I, 5, 1, 1.

Tseng's Comment

"As we cut, as we file," refers to the intelligent method of study; "As we carve the jade and grind it" refers to the self-discipline; "Firm in decision, on guard against calumny and its makers" indicates his anxiety to be fair; "Splendid, his voice our impulse" indicates his stern equity in the halls of judgment; "A prince of many talents, who will carry through to the end, who will not go back on his word" indicates that style of conduct offered as the

道盛德至善民之不能忘
也詩云於戲前王不忘君
子賢其賢而親其親小人
樂其樂而利其利此以沒
世不忘也子曰聽訟吾猶
人也必也使無訟乎無情

grain to the gods, without blemish, total in rectitude, and this the people cannot forget.

Tseng's Comment

5.

The *Odes* say:

In our ceremonial plays,
In the ritual dances
with tiger masks and spears
The archetype kings are not forgotten.

—*Shi King*, IV, 1, 4, 3.

The great gentlemen honor the worth they honored and hold in attentive affection the growing and ordered things which they held in affection; the lesser folk delight in that wherein the ancient kings delighted and profit by what profited them [their canals and good customs]; thus the generations pass like water and the former kings are not forgotten.

This is the third chapter of the comment sifting out the grist of the phrase: be at ease in total rectitude.

Whether the ideogram indicating distinctions, which Legge translates "former," starts out by indicating a cutting of meat after hunting or a measuring of the different slices of the moon astronomically, I cannot say, nor do I remember whether Karlgren has an opinion on it.

止於至善

IV

Kung said: In hearing law-suits I am no worse than anyone else, but one should eliminate law-suits. If the not quite candid were

者不得盡其辭大畏民志
此謂知本此謂知本此謂
知之至也所謂誠其意者
毋自欺也如惡惡臭如好
好色此之謂自謙故君子
必慎其獨也小人閒居爲

unable to pour out their rhetoric to the full, a greater awe and respect [for government justice] would prevail in the popular mind. This is called knowing the root.

This is the fourth chapter of the comment giving the gist of the remark (in the Confucian canon) about the root and the branch.

V

This is called knowing the root.
This is called completing the cognitions.

知之至

There is here a lacuna in place of the fifth chapter of the comment. Ch'eng's speculation about it was not essential to E. P.'s earlier edition and is not in the Stone-Classics as the reader can see for himself.

VI

1.

Finding the precise word for the inarticulate heart's tone means not lying to oneself, as in the case of hating a bad smell or loving a beautiful person, also called respecting one's own nose.

On this account the real man has to look his heart in the eye even when he is alone.

2.

There is, for the small man living unobserved,

不善無所不至見君子而
后厭然揜其不善而著其
善人之視己如見其肺肝
然則何益矣此謂誠於中
形於外故君子必慎其獨
也曾子曰十目所視十手

no iniquity that he will not carry through to the limit; if he sees a true man he turns and takes cover, hides his iniquities, sticks out his merits, but the other fellow sees the significance of this as if he saw into his lungs and liver; what is the good of his faking, what dish does it cover?

Tseng's Comment

That is the meaning of the saying: the true word is in the middle inside and will show on the outside. Therefore the man of real breeding who carries the cultural and moral heritage must look his heart in the eye when alone.

3.

Tseng Tsze said: what ten eyes gaze at, what ten hands

所指其嚴乎富潤屋德潤
身心廣體胖故君子必誠
其意所謂脩身在正其心
者身有所忿懥則不得其
正有所恐懼則不得其正
有所好樂則不得其正有

point to should preserve a certain decorum [ought to be mentionable, discussable].

Tseng's Comment

4.

You improve the old homestead by material riches and irrigation; you enrich and irrigate the character by the process of looking straight into the heart and then acting on the results. Thus the mind becomes your palace and the body can be at ease; it is for this reason that the great gentleman must find the precise verbal expression for his inarticulate thoughts.

This is the sixth chapter of the comment, sorting out the grist of the sentence about finding precise verbal expression for the heart's tone, for the inarticulate thoughts.

The dominant ideograms in the chapter are the sun's lance falling true on the word, and the heart giving off tone.

誠意

VII

1.

In the phrase, "Self discipline is rooted in rectification of the heart," the word rectify (*cheng*) can be illustrated as follows: if there be a knife of resentment in the heart or enduring rancor, the mind will not attain precision; under suspicion and fear it will not form sound judgment, nor will it, dazzled by love's delight

所憂患則不得其正心不在焉視而不見聽而不聞食而不知其味此謂脩身在正其心所謂齊其家在脩其身者人之其所親愛而辟焉之其所賤惡而辟

nor in sorrow and anxiety, come to precisions.

Tseng's Comment

2.

If the heart have not stable root, eager for justice, one looks and sees not [looks and sees phantoms]; listens and hears not [listens internally and does not hear objectively]; eats and knows not the flavors.

That is what we mean by saying: self-discipline is rooted in rectifying the heart.

正心脩身

This is the seventh chapter of the commentary giving the gist of: "rectifying the heart disciplines the character."

As to the frequent lack of tense indications, the ideogramic mind assumes that what has been, is and will be. Only the exception, or the sequence of events requires further indications. See also verse 3 of the canon.

VIII

1.

The phrase, "Regulation of the family is rooted in self-discipline," can be understood by observing that men love what they see growing up under their own roof, and show partiality; if they have something in contempt and hate it, they are partial;

焉之其所畏敬而辟焉之
其所哀矜而辟焉之其所
敖惰而辟焉故好而知其
惡惡而知其美者天下鮮
矣故諺有之曰人莫知其
子之惡莫知其苗之碩此

if they are filled with reverence and respect, they are partial; if they feel sorrow and compassion, they are partial; and then someone comes arrogantly along paying no attention to us, and our judgment of them is thereby influenced. There are, thus, few men under heaven who can love and see the defects, or hate and see the excellence of an object.

Tseng's Comment

2.

Hence the shaggy proverb: No man knows his son's faults, no one knows the stone-hard grain in the stalk's head from the first sprouts.

謂身不脩不可以齊其家
所謂治國必先齊其家者
其家不可教而能教人者
無之故君子不出家而成
教於國孝者所以事君也
弟者所以事長也慈者所

3.

That is the meaning of the saying: If a man does not discipline himself he cannot bring order into the home.

Tseng's Comment

This is the eighth chapter of the comment dealing with self-discipline and domestic order.

IX

1.

What is meant by saying, "To govern a state one must first bring order into one's family," is this: the man who, being incapable of educating his own family, is able to educate other men just doesn't exist. On which account the real man perfects the nation's culture without leaving his fireside. There, at home, is the filial sense whereby a prince is served; there the fraternal deference that serves in relations to one's elders and to those in higher grade; there the kindness in matters of detail that is needed

以使衆也康誥曰如保赤
子心誠求之雖不中不
遠矣未有學養子而后嫁
者也一家仁一國興仁一
家讓一國興讓一人貪戾
一國作亂其機如此此謂

in dealing with the mass of people.

Tseng's Comment

2.

The K'ang Proclamation says: "As if taking care of an infant." If the heart sincerely wants to, although one may not hit the mark precisely in the center, one won't go far wrong. No girl ever yet studied suckling a baby in order to get married.

3.

One humane family can humanize a whole state; one courteous family can lift a whole state into courtesy; one grasping and perverse man can drive a nation to chaos. Such are the seeds of movement [*semina motuum*, the inner impulses of the tree]. That is what we mean by:

一言僨事一人定國堯舜
率天下以仁而民從之桀
紂率天下以暴而民從之
其所令反其所好而民不
從是故君子有諸己而后
求諸人無諸己而后非諸

one word will ruin the business, one man can bring the state to an orderly course.

Tseng's Comment

4.

Yau and Shun led the empire by their humanity and the people followed; Chieh and Chou governed the empire with overweening violence and the people copied their conduct, their imperial orders being in contradiction to their likes, the people did not follow the orders.

Whence we note that the prince must have in himself not one but all of the qualities that he requires from others, and must himself be empty of what he does not want from others in reflex.

人所藏乎身不恕而能喻
諸人者未之有也故治國
在齊其家詩云桃之夭夭
其葉蓁蓁之子于歸宜
其家人宜其家人而后可
以教國人詩云宜兄宜弟

No one has ever yet been able to induct others into a style of conduct not part of his own viscera.

Tseng's Comment

5.

That is why the government of a state is rooted in keeping order in one's own family.

6.

The *Odes* say:

Delicate as the peach-tree in blossom
The leaves abundant as grass-blades,
Fragile fair she goes
to the house of her husband,
The bride who will bring harmony to it
As an altar raised on earth
under heaven.

—*Shi King*, I, 1, 6, 3.

As an altar bringing harmony and order into the home. Given that, one can teach the people throughout the state.

7.

The *Odes* say:

In harmony with heaven above
And with earth below
The elder and younger brothers
About an altar, in harmony.

—*Shi King*, II, 2, 9, 3.

When there is this harmony between elder and younger brothers you can educate the men of the nation.

宜兄宜弟而后可以教國
人詩云其儀不忒正是四
國其爲父子兄弟足法而
后民法之也此謂治國在
齊其家所謂平天下在治
其國者上老老而民興孝

8.

The *Odes* say:

He practiced equity without
its making him feel
That a javelin were being
thrust into his heart.

—*Shi King*, I, 14, 3, 3.

Tseng's Comment

[*Aliter*, faultlessly.] On these lines he rectified the state to its four angles. When right conduct between father and son, between brother and younger brother, has become sufficiently instinctive, the people will follow the course as ruled.

9.

That is the meaning of: The government of the state is rooted in family order.

This is the ninth chapter of the comment giving the gist of: Put order in the home in order to govern the country.

X

1.

The meaning of, "World Order [bringing what is under heaven into equilibrium] is rooted in the good government of one's own state," is this: If those in high place respect the aged, the people will bring filial piety to a high level;

上長長而民興弟上恤孤
而民不倍是以君子有絜
矩之道也所惡於上毋以使
下所惡於下毋以事上所
惡於前毋以先後所惡於
後毋以從前所惡於右毋

以交於左所惡於左毋以
交於右此之謂絜矩之道
詩云樂只君子民之父母
民之所好好之民之所惡
惡之此之謂民之父母詩
云節彼南山維石巖巖赫

if those in high place show deference to their elders, the people will bring their fraternal deference to a high level; if those in high place pity orphans, the people will not do otherwise; it is by this that the great gentlemen have a guide to conduct, a compass and square of the process.

Tseng's Comment

2.

If you hate something in your superiors, do not practice it on those below you; if you hate a thing in those below you, do not do it when working for those over you. If you hate something in the man ahead of you, do not do it to the fellow who follows you; if a thing annoy you from the man at your heels, do not push it at the man in front of you.

Do not in your relations with your left-hand neighbor what annoys you if done at your right, nor in your relations to your right-hand neighbor what annoys you if done at your left. This is callcd having a compass and T-square of the process.

Tseng's Comment

3.

The *Odes* say:

What a joy are these princes
At once father and mother
of their people.
—*Shi King*, II, 2, 5, 3.

To love what the people love and hate what is bad for the people [what they hate] is called being the people's father and mother.

4.

The *Odes* say:

South Mountain
Cutting the horizon, fold over fold,
Steep cliffs full of voices and echoes,
Towering over the echoes,
Towering;

赫師尹民具爾瞻有國者
不可以不慎辟則爲天下
僇矣詩云殷之未喪師克
配上帝儀監于殷峻命不
易道得衆則得國失衆則
失國是故君子先慎乎德

Resplendent, resplendent,
Yin, Lord Conductor,
The people gaze at you,
muttering under their breath.
—*Shi King*, II, 4, 7, 1.
(Chia-fu's invective against Yin)

Tseng's Comment

Those who have rule over states and families cannot but look themselves straight in the heart; if they deviate they bring shame on the whole empire.

5.

The *Odes* say:

Until the Yin had lost the assembly . . .
They could offer the cup and drink with
The Most Highest.

—*Shi King*, III, 1, 1, 6.

We can measure our regard for equity by the Yin. High destiny is not easy. Right action gains the people* and that gives one the state. Lose the people, you lose the state.

6.

Therefore the great gentleman starts by looking straight into his heart to see how he is getting on with the process of acting

* I think this ideogram has an original sense of the people gathered at its tribal blood rite.

有德此有人有人此有土
有土此有財有財此有用
德者本也財者末也外本
內末爭民施奪是故財聚
則民散財散則民聚是故
言悖而出者亦悖而入貨

on the basis of such direct observation. When he can see and act straight in this, he will have the people with him; having the people, he will have the territory; having the land, the product will be under his control, and controling this wealth he will have the means to act and make use of it.

Tseng's Comment

7.

The *virtu*, i.e., this self-knowledge [looking straight into the heart and acting thence] is the root; the wealth is a by-product.

8.

If you leave the root in the open and plant the branch, you will merely embroil the people and lead them to robbing hen-roosts.

9.

Rake in wealth and you scatter the people. Divide the wealth and the people will gather to you.

10.

Words that go out a-wry, pettishly, will return as turmoil,

悖而入者亦悖而出康誥
曰惟命不于常道善則得
之不善則失之矣楚書曰
楚國無以爲寶惟善以爲
寶舅犯曰亡人無以爲寶
仁親以爲寶秦誓曰若有

and as for money: ill got, ill go.

Tseng's Comment

11.

The K'ang Proclamation has said: Heaven's decree is not given in permanence: Proceeding with rightness you attain it, and with unrightness spew it away.

12.

In the Ch'u History it is said: The Ch'u state does not go in for collecting wealth [treasuring porcelain, jewels and money] but counts fair-dealing* its treasure.

13.

Uncle Fan (refusing an offer of bribery) said: The lost man [King Wen in exile] does not treasure jewels and such wealth, counting his manhood and the love of his relatives the true treasure.

14.

It is said in the Ch'in Declaration: If I had

* Legge says "its good men."

一个臣斷斷兮無他技其
心休休焉其如有容焉人
之有技若己有之人之彦
聖其心好之不啻若自其
口出寔能容之以能保我
子孫黎民尚亦有利哉人

but one straight minister who could cut the cackle [ideogram of the ax and the documents of the archives tied up in silk], yes, if without other abilities save simple honesty, a moderate spender but having the magnanimity to recognize talent in others, it would be as if he himself had those talents; and when others had erudition and wisdom he would really like it and love them, not merely talk about it and make a show from the mouth outward but solidly respect them, and be able to stand having talented men about him; such a man could sustain my sons and descendents and the black-haired people, and benefits would mount up from him.

Tseng's Comment

之有技媢疾以惡之人之
彥聖而違之俾不通寔不
能容以不能保我子孫黎
民亦曰殆哉唯仁人放流
之迸諸四夷不與同中國
此謂唯仁人爲能愛人能

Tseng's Comment

But if, when others have ability, he acts like a jealous female sick with envy, and hates them; and if, when others have knowledge and sage judgment, he shoves them out of the way and prevents their promotion and just can't stand 'em when they have real worth, he will *not* preserve my sons and grandsons and the Chinese people, in fact he can be called a real pest.

15.

Only the fully humane man will throw out such a minister and send him off among the barbarians of the frontiers. He will not associate with him in the Middle Kingdom; that is what is meant by: Only the fully humane man can love another; or can

惡人見賢而不能舉舉而
不能先命也見不善而不
能退退而不能遠過也好
人之所惡惡人之所好是
謂拂人之性菑必逮夫身
是故君子有大道必忠信

really hate him.

16.

Tseng's Comment

To see high merit and be unable to raise it to office, to raise it but not to give such promotion precedence, is just destiny; to see iniquity and not have the capacity to throw it out; to throw it out and not have the capacity to send it to distant exile, is to err.

17.

To love what the people hate, to hate what they love is called doing violence to man's inborn nature. Calamities will come to him who does this [definite physical calamities], the wild grass will grow over his dead body.

18.

Thus the true man has his great mode of action which must be from the plumb center of his heart, maintaining his given word

以得之驕泰以失之生財
有大道生之者衆食之者
寡爲之者疾用之者舒則
財恒足矣仁者以財發身
不仁者以身發財未有上
好仁而下不好義者也未

that he come to his deed in due hour. Pride and jactancy lose all this.

Tseng's Comment

19.

And there is a chief way for the production of wealth, namely, that the producers be many and that the mere consumers be few; that the artisan mass be energetic and the consumers temperate, then the constantly circulating goods will be always a-plenty.*

20.

"Good king is known by his spending, ill lord by his taking." The humane man uses his wealth as a means to distinction, the inhumane becomes a mere harness, an accessory to his takings.

21.

There has never been in high place a lover of the human qualities, of full manhood, but that those below him loved equity.

---

* I think the ideogram indicates not only a constant circulation of goods but also a sort of alluvial deposit all along the course of the circuit.

有好義其事不終者也未
有府庫財非其財者也
孟獻子曰畜馬乘不察於
雞豚伐冰之家不畜牛羊
百乘之家不畜聚斂之臣
與其有聚斂之臣寧有盜

Never have such lovers of equity failed to carry through their work to completion, nor have the treasures in such a ruler's libraries and arsenals not been used to his benefit and stayed his.

Tseng's Comment

22.

The official, Meng Hsien, said: Men who keep horses and carriages do not tend fowls and pigs; a family that uses ice in its ancestral ceremonies does not run a cattle and sheep farm; one having a fief of a hundred war chariots does not maintain a minister to clap people into the Black Maria [for non-payment of unjust taxes]. Rather than have a minister who claps people into the police van [nefariously] it would be better to have one who robs the state funds.

臣此謂國不以利爲利以
義爲利也長國家而務財
用者必自小人矣彼爲善
之小人之使爲國家菑害
並至雖有善者亦無如之
何矣此謂國不以利爲利

That is the significance of the phrase: a country does not profit by making profits, its equity is its profit.

Tseng's Comment

23.

When the head of a state or family thinks first of gouging out an income, he must perforce do it through small men; and even if they are clever at their job, if one employ such inferior characters in state and family business the tilled fields will go to rack swamp and ruin and edged calamities will mount up to the full; and even if, thereafter, an honest man be brought into the administration he will not be then able to find remedy for these ills.

That is the meaning of:
A state does not profit by profits.

以義爲利也

禮記卷第十九

Honesty is the treasure of states.

Tseng's Comment

The old commentator ends by saying: "Despise not this comment because of its simplicity."

The translator would end by asking the reader to keep on re-reading the whole digest until he understands HOW these few pages contain the basis on which the great dynasties were founded and endured, and why, lacking this foundation, the other and lesser dynasties perished quickly.

D.T.C., Pisa;
5 October—5 November, 1945.

"We are at the crisis point
of the world."

—Tami Kume, 1924.

國、不以利爲利、以義爲利也

"EQUITY
IS
THE
TREASURE
OF
STATES"

CHUNG YUNG
THE UNWOBBLING PIVOT

NOTE

The second of the Four Classics, Chung Yung, *THE UNWOBBLING PIVOT*, contains what is usually supposed not to exist, namely the Confucian metaphysics. It is divided into three parts: the axis; the process; and sincerity, the perfect word, or the precise word; into

Metaphysics:

Only the most absolute sincerity under heaven can effect any change.

Politics:

In cutting an axe-handle the model is not far off, in this sense: one holds one axe-handle while chopping the other. Thus one uses men in governing men.

Ethics:

The archer, when he misses the bullseye, turns and seeks the cause of the error in himself.

CHU HSI'S PREFACE

My master the philosopher Ch'eng says: The word *chung* signifies what is bent neither to one side nor to the other. The word *yung* signifies unchanging. What exists plumb in the middle is the just process of the universe and that which never wavers or wobbles is the calm principle operant in its mode of action.

The spirit of this work comes from the door of Confucius, the heart's law transmitted *viva voce* from master to pupil, memorized and talked back and forth as mutual control of the invariable modus of action. Tsze Sze, fearing that with the passage of time the tradition might be distorted, wrote it out on the bamboo tablets and thus it came down to Mencius.

At its start the book speaks of the one principle, it then spreads into a discussion of things in general, and concludes by uniting all this in the one principle. Spread it out and its arrows reach to the six ends of the universe, zenith and nadir; fold it again and it withdraws to serve you in secret as faithful minister. Its savour is inexhaustible. It is, all of it, solid wisdom. The fortunate and attentive reader directing his mind to the solid, delighting in it as in a gem always carried, penetrating into its mysterious purity, when he has come to meridian, to the precise understanding, can use it till the end of his life, never exhausting it, never able to wear it out.

禮記卷第十六

中庸第卅一　　禮記

鄭氏注

天命之謂性率性之謂道

脩道之謂教道也者不可

PART ONE

TSZE SZE'S FIRST THESIS

I

1.

What heaven has disposed and sealed is called the inborn nature. The realization of this nature is called the process. The clarification of this process [the understanding or making intelligible of this process] is called education.

Note by Chu Hsi, an eleventh century commentator: The preceding is the first chapter in which Tsze Sze presents the tradition of the thought as the basis of his discourse. The main thing is to illumine the root of the process, a fountain of clear water descending from heaven immutable. The components, the bones of things, the materials are implicit and prepared in us, abundant and inseparable from us.*

Tsze Sze then speaks of the necessity of watching, nourishing, examining and re-examining them seriously and concludes by speaking of the way in which the spiritual nature of the sage carries his transmuting and operant power

(*Continued on page* 95)

* Cf. Shi King, III, 3, 6, 7.

須臾離也可離非道也是
故君子戒慎乎其所不睹
恐懼乎其所不聞莫見乎
隱莫顯乎微故君子慎其
獨也喜怒哀樂之未發謂
之中發而皆中節謂之和